CONFLICT
RESOLUTION

BISHOP TUDOR BISMARK

Published by C4Promotions

Contact Lisa Jenkins-Moore
www.c4promotions.com

Content Development provided by Remnant Word Publishing Company.
Contact Shaunta D. Scroggins at serious_remnant@hotmail.com for more information.

To order additional copies of this resource or other resources, please visit our website at www.tudorbismark.org.uk

Printed in the United States of America

ISBN 10: 147522978X

ISBN 13: 9781475229783

CONTENTS

INTRODUCTION

Discovering methods to best resolve conflict in ministry settings is about one thing: improvement. Regardless of attained success levels, each leader has a responsibility to seasonally focus on assessing systems for the purpose of improvement toward greater Kingdom effectiveness. Improvement affords the ministry the opportunity to successfully track and account for growth.

Improvement opportunities include but are not limited to: Bible studies, workshops, seminars or conferences. Within these opportunities, succession planning must be addressed as inter-ministry relationships mature and advance and securing an exit strategy is imperative. An exit strategy protects the leader, the ministry, the current members and the departing individuals and is a key component in conflict resolution.

Conflict is inspired by our enemy, the devil, and walked out through human beings. It has the potential to destroy not only individual lives, but also local churches. Conflict accompanies a level of division and destruction from which some never recover. We understand that differences occur because we as human beings are diverse. There are multi-level diversities in every area of human existence so the potential for conflict always exists. We hope this series will provide practical wisdom from our years in ministry service that will teach pastors, leaders and lay members to identify and stand in sober defense against the enemy's devices.

ONE: CATEGORIES OF CONFLICT

But I urge and entreat you, brethren, by the name of our Lord Jesus Christ, that all of you be in perfect harmony and full agreement in what you say, and that there be no dissensions or factions or divisions among you, but that you be perfectly united in your common understanding and in your opinions and judgments.

1 Corinthians 1:10 (AMP)

CONFLICT DEFINED

The popular definitions of conflict include a competitive or opposing action of incompatibles; mental struggle resulting from incompatible or opposing needs, drives, wishes or external or internal demands; the opposition of persons or forces that gives rise to the dramatic action in a drama or fiction.[1]

Look closely at the last definition: the opposition of persons or forces that gives rise to dramatic action. That is the nature of conflict. If left unchecked, conflict causes drama in the ministry. What is drama? Drama is a state, situation, or series of events involving interesting or intense conflict of forces.[2]

Take a few moments to consider your life and connections. Is there drama in any relationship or area of your life? In your ministry? If so, it most likely can be traced back to conflict. Regardless of size or scope, conflict is powerful and can damage and devastate God's people. Conflict is often fueled by spoken words—James 3:5 summarizes the tongue's role in conflict: *Even so the tongue is a little member, and it can boast of great things. See how much wood or how great a forest a tiny spark can set ablaze!* (AMP)

SIX MAJOR CAUSES OF CONFLICT

We will address six major causes of conflict in ministry: subcultures and abusive systems, lack of integrity in money matters, moral problems, lack of an exit strategy, jealousy among gifted people, and neglect of social needs.

Subcultures

Subcultures form when pastors allow leaders to develop their own departments or ministries with little supervision. Without pastoral oversight, cliques may emerge. What begins as a teambuilding tea or dinner morphs into secret societies and exclusive relationships. It is possible for pastors to identify subcultures early. Once identified, it is important that the subculture be defused, dismantled and rearranged into the corporate overall vision of the ministry. No leadership style in ministry is exempt from the possibilities of "sub-cultures" developing. Any progressive ministry within itself possesses the capabilities to raise up competent dynamic leaders. The danger is that these leaders in turn may create a "sub-culture" where they build people, ideas, and concepts around themselves and not around the "Set Leader" and the vision of the house.

Abusive Systems

Abusive systems are not just harsh or oppressive systems, but antagonistic environments that tend to abuse, exploit, misuse, manipulate or oppress people. According to Dr. Samuel Chand, a person can have a perfectly good anointing or gift but be located in a toxic environment. This toxic environment has within in it the possibilities of abuse, misconduct, and inappropriate behaviors, structures and systems. There are four components that contribute to abusive systems.

First, there is the lack of personal development within the leader. When the leader refuses to deal with personal issues, establish personal discipline, or better himself / herself, an abusive system can be created. As a result the leader will possibly mistreat members of the leadership and congregation. The weaknesses and incompetence's of the leader are then imposed on the ministry, thus creating conflict.

Second, there are problems with appointed leaders. Frontline, handpicked pastoral team members may have personal issues that cause conflict among the congregation.

Third, there is lack of communication among the leaders or to the congregation, due to insufficient direction or vision conveyed from the pastor.

Fourth, there are unresolved theological and cultural belief systems; then the belief is imposed on a church, or ministry without discussion, or thought of immediate consequence. Some "cultural beliefs" can become abusive as they pertain to dictatorial, demagogue style force, causing conflict due to the unbalanced beliefs.

Lack of Integrity in Money Matters

There are innumerable church conflicts that stem from money issues.

Whether the problem is theft, mismanagement, or misappropriation, the solution is accountability. There must be transparency in the ministry's finances, so that the leaders are unable to "skim off the top." In addition, the financial requirements imposed on ministers and churches must not be unreasonable, or this too can cause conflict.

Values Differences

A church should be built on strong, clearly defined Biblical values. These values should be succinctly expressed and should be in writing. Having specified values within the congregation births family and spiritual standards that influence society. Entrepreneurs, politicians and leaders representing every sector in society can spring from the church, so it is essential that the church has core character strengths that are clearly defined. When the church has clearly defined its values, there is no question on its position.

Value issues also take into account doctrinal, cultural, racial, and political differences. Various people groupings around the world, in individual nations tribally, and in communities racially (blacks and whites) act and think differently. Americans and those from other countries believe differently. Pastors must use wisdom when multi-cultural factors are present. Remain apolitical. It may prove beneficial to conduct a doctrinal audit so that everyone in the ministry can be on the same page about specific methods the church employs. Topics may range from baptismal methods to the administration of the sacraments.

Lack of an Exit Strategy

There is always someone in the ministry who believes they can do it better—planning, singing, preaching, etc. For this reason it is imperative that churches have an exit strategy. This is a simple set of procedures to help gifted people transition into starting their own works while still preserving the unity of the church.

Though some people leave a church without anger or malice, unnecessary conflict is created when they leave, or attempt to leave because an exit strategy does not exist. Following are various scenarios of why people leave a church / ministry: 1) People leave because employment, or relocate because of accommodation within the same city another city or another country etc; 2) people in good standing who feel / sense they need to change churches for some reason (and there are a variety of reasons) 3) people not in good standing who wish to change churches and/or ministries 4) members or employees in good standing that need to change departments or ministries and 5) problematic people that need to move on. An exit strategy needs to be written documentation that describes the exact procedure used to deal with common situations. Having an exit strategy in place is essential to starting a church or ministry.

Jealousy Among Gifted People

If your church has fifty-three gifted ministers within the assembly, it will be difficult for any one of them to get the necessary training and exposure they need to be fully productive. Even if each minister preached one week out of the year, you would still come up one week short! Senior pastors must make a concentrated effort to train, mentor and create opportunities for the gifted people in the ministry. Do not ignore gifts and talents, cultivate them. Recognizing gifts and callings and creating a nurturing environment for them will prevent people from competing for positions in the spotlight and help avoid conflict.

Neglect of Social Needs

People within the church are given to different passions and feel strongly about certain organizations and charities. Some will focus on the poor or the homeless; others will champion a different cause. If a church fails to demonstrate the same level of passion that some do for their cause, this can be a source of conflict. Have a plan in place that demonstrates the churches commitment to its community.

TWO: TYPES OF CONFLICT

"I encourage leaders to locate all potential areas of conflict and close those doors. Then look for the conflicts you have no control over."

Bishop Tudor Bismark

But immorality (sexual vice) and all impurity [of lustful, rich, wasteful living] or greediness must not even be named among you, as is fitting and proper among saints (God's consecrated people). Let there be no filthiness (obscenity, indecency) nor foolish and sinful (silly and corrupt) talk, nor coarse jesting, which are not fitting or becoming; but instead voice your thankfulness [to God].

Ephesians 5:3–4 (AMP)

Foreseeing and properly handling conflict helps a growing ministry maintain momentum. Momentum can be lost almost instantly when major conflict arises. Assess weak areas and close the doors to possible conflict to ensure growth. Within each of the six aforementioned conflict categories there are many possible causes for the conflict. We will briefly address the five major types of conflicts, including examples where appropriate. Please note that this list is in order of the most obvious causes of conflict.

SEXUAL SIN

Sexual sin is the most obvious attack, and the one for which leaders are most unprepared. Conflict breaks out in a ministry when there is sexual sin, and it usually occurs in categories. The first is within church leadership (that is, the set man, the set woman, or the first family). Immediately under them are their respective leadership teams. Below this level are second-line or third-line leaders of departments (this includes all areas of ministry: children, media, music, men, women, and so on).

Regardless of who commits sexual sin, many are affected. Whether leaders commit this sin with other leaders inside the church, other members in the assembly not in leadership, or those that are outside the church, it can create problems for everyone. Many high profile ministries have lost everything seemingly overnight because a leader slept with another leader, a congregant, or someone outside of the church. This sinful behavior has the potential to split churches, and some people never recover—from senior leadership on down to the membership. Sexual sin will destroy a church and cause a marvelous move of God to be broken.

I know of a church that built significant momentum; the pastor was well known and the worship leader was premier in the entire region. When it was alleged that the worship leader had had an affair with one of the elders, the momentum came to a halt within a month. The pastor was later arrested and falsely accused of unethical dealings, all stemming from this attack involving the worship leader.

Do not keep sexual sin a secret because it will feed the rumor mill. Presenting the truth immediately is far better than trying to repair the damage done by secrets and exaggerated gossip.

FINANCIAL CONFLICT

One of the biggest causes of financial conflict is the mismanagement and/ or misappropriation of funds. If a ministry holds a capital campaign for building renovation then the money should not be spent on choir robes. When money is publicly earmarked and dedicated for a specific purpose, it should be used for that purpose. Pastors should be publicly accountable for the church financial position and any major purchase decisions. Financial clarity and disciplined spending can prevent many problems from occurring.

Leaders in my part of the world tend to live beyond their means. Eventually they start living off members of their congregation. This behavior has to stop and must be avoided at all costs.

Have formal financial records in place and perform an annual audit. I recommend avoiding business dealings with members. Eliminate inappropriate systems.

EMOTIONAL PROBLEMS

People with serious emotional issues have many triggers. It can be dangerous to have people with emotional problems serving in the church because one may not know when they will erupt. The easy route is to cast them aside with harsh verbal reprimand. A pastor short on patience can inflict further wounds and teeter on abusing these people through direct rebuke or indirect suggestion over the pulpit. A better way to deal with individuals with emotional issues is to arrange counseling and help them determine a course for healing. For leaders, this course is mandatory. Remove struggling individuals from any leadership post while they heal and allow them to demonstrate emotional stability before re-instating them.

ORGANIZATIONAL STRUCTURES

When there is a lack of vision or unclear vision in a church there is a revolving door. Strategic thinkers questioning the vision come across as challenging the leader. Gather teams to help develop the vision. If not, someone in the ministry will form a pseudo-vision, draw people to it, and mislead the ministry.

Consider Exodus 24:12–18. Moses was on the mountain getting instructions from God. Aaron was below creating a contrary system because he did not have a clear understanding of the vision (Exodus 32:1–6).

Unclear organizational structures bring a lack of definition. Conflict is created when authority and accountability is not clearly defined. People clash with varying opinions, and eventually stronger willed people will continue to push the line to see how far they can go. There should be a framework structure and systems to be revisited regularly to accommodate ministry growth.

A lack of rewards or an imbalance in rewards creates conflict. The lack of job descriptions creates conflict because no one knows who reports to whom. This is seen when pastors appoint leaders without clear task assignments or when full time staffers are uncertain about their duties. A lack of descriptions opens the door to pastors exercising a double standard in judgments in how problem-causers are disciplined. I recommend eliminating confusion and double standards by creating a code of conduct.

LACK OF MATURITY IN THE BODY OF CHRIST

Immaturity brings conflict and divides the church. Immature people do not recognize the need for the supernatural. They have a problem enduring difficult seasons. They resort to fault finding, bad mouthing the pastor, and pointing blame. Immature people do not realize that the responsibility is on them (not just the pastor) to release manifestations of God's power.

THREE: SCENARIOS OF CONFLICT

"Every action in a ministry is a teaching opportunity."

Bishop Tudor Bismark

Now, let's discuss the various scenarios of conflict. I want to offer basic recommendations in line with the suggested pattern of general discipline.

WITH THE UNSAVED

If a member of the church is in conflict with an unbeliever or if a pastor is in conflict with an outside person, both member and pastor must behave in a Christ-like way. They must act like Christians. If taken to court, I recommend pastors stand with their member for protection if he or she was obedient and compliant to the law. If the member disobeyed the law, was in contravention of the law, then the said member must make right even if he / she is taken to court.

AN AGGRIEVED MEMBER

The member works first with the pastoral team for clarification. Depending on the offense, there may be a need for a witness. The pastoral team works with the offended person. Consider appointing a Grievance Committee and putting a church policy into writing. Only in the case of escalation does the grievance need to be handled by the senior pastor.

WITHIN AND AMONG THE CONGREGATION

Sadly, grievances among church members are a reality. Allow the pastoral teams to handle these issues. If the situation escalates, there should be a meeting in the pastor's office and resolution attempted according to the set standard (i.e., the code of conduct). Further measures could include a disciplinary committee and a discussion of a written record by letter. Ultimately, if there can be no resolution, the member finds a new church.

AMONG PASTORS, BISHOPS AND SENIOR CHURCH LEADERSHIP

Within a local church, the offended leader should initiate the meeting with the senior pastor. If no reconciliation is possible, then the offended leader should step down. An arbitration team should meet with the offended leader in cases of conflict between any member of the staff and the senior leader.

Conflict among pastoral leaders of different congregations requires a wider net to be cast for resolution. Depending on the conflict, a team of generally respected senior pastors in the city should be called in to arbitrate.

WITH THE SENIOR PASTOR AND FIRST LADY

In cases of dramatic conflict heading toward the separation in marriage and/or ministry, the apostolic covering or oversight should be brought in to provide leadership to the pastor, pastor's wife and the congregants. This kind of conflict is dangerous because it inhibits moves of the Holy Spirit and it causes "camps" to arise. The people end up in three groups: pro him, pro her, and the middle ground people who do not like the entire conflict.

As a senior pastor, the key is to have the right code of conduct, the right leadership structure, and the right people above you to properly address conflicts. You cannot control criticism that is on the outside. Your responsibility is to keep a healthy church environment. As an under shepherd, make sure the sheep are healthy; lead them to green pastures and beside still waters. Protect correspondence with witnesses.

FOUR: A GENERAL PATTERN OF DISCIPLINE

The law of the Lord is perfect, restoring the [whole] person; the testimony of the Lord is sure, making wise the simple. The precepts of the Lord are right, rejoicing the heart; the commandment of the Lord is pure and bright, enlightening the eyes. The [reverent] fear of the Lord is clean, enduring forever; the ordinances of the Lord are true and righteous altogether.

Psalm 19:7–9 (AMP)

We recommend a general pattern of corrective action for conflict that is applicable across various scenarios, such as those discussed in the next section. At the top of the list is the existence and active use of a ministry code of conduct. This is a document where, in writing, leaders clearly communicate expectations of members and congregants when aligning with the belief system and ideologies of the ministry.

There have been cases where in the absence of a Code of Conduct, double standards exist. For example, in a ministry some years ago, a member of the church fell to sexual sin, became pregnant and was then severely dealt with by the leadership. She set down for a year, limited her communication with members of the church, made an apology to the leadership, and then to the congregation, and had to endure a very hurtful backlash from the church and leadership as a whole. Three years later the Pastor's daughter fell into exactly the same situation. A quick quiet wedding was arranged, nothing was said, no apologies made. There was a masterful cover-up to save the Pastor's and Church's embarrassment. The Pastor's daughter was not required to make an apology on any level, and resumed work in the ministry and leadership shortly after her honeymoon. Clearly a double standard existed in this situation and might have been avoided had a ministry code of conduct been in place and executed in BOTH situations.

CODE OF CONDUCT

The Code of Conduct is a simple document, customized to fit the operation of a ministry that explains who you are, what you are called to do, how you are called to do it, and the guidelines around doing it. If the ministry is a local church, then each family should have a copy so that everyone is aware of processes and procedures. That way, when conflict arises everyone can refer to the common code of conduct. It is a community document, written for and to serve the interests of the community—those present now and those who are to come.

Document what is to be done if any of the sins described in the previous section come up. Consider both parties who committed the sin.

MINOR WARNING

All letters are teachable opportunities. Curb the "dictator desire" to lash out, pull rank, and cause further damage. The minor warning, the first step, is a formal letter clearly describing the problem and addressing it as unacceptable. If addressed to a leader, all of this person's leadership functions are suspended as a form of discipline. This establishes a paper trail, a documented procedural pattern on how to confront a problem and leaves open the possibilities of restoration.

SEVERE WARNING

The severe warning is issued with church elders as a final warning to repent.

FINAL WARNING & EX-COMMUNICATION

The final warning is absolutely the last option. If implementing this level of discipline, my recommendation is to consult the legal counsel for the church to ensure protection from law suits. High level counsel can be (depending on the ministry's organizational structures and government) consulting the Apostolic leadership of the ministry or covering, or Eldership appointed above the ministry, or collective College of Bishops or Presbyters, or District Elders etc. Also consultation from peer leaders that are unrelated to the problem so that an unbiased view with recommendations can be presented. There may need to be legal counsel to protect the Leadership and the interests of the church or ministry.

Always consider the other family members of a person in the discipline process who want to remain in fellowship at the church. Extend grace every time.

Brothers, if someone is caught in a sin, you who are spiritual should restore him gently. But watch yourself, or you also may be tempted. Carry each other's burdens, and in this way you will fulfill the law of Christ.

Galatians 6:1–2 (NIV)

FIVE: RESOLVING CONFLICT

So that there should be no division or discord or lack of adaptation [of the parts of the body to each other], but the members all alike should have a mutual interest in and care for one another.

1 Corinthians 12:25 (AMP)

The Scriptures give counsel on how to resolve conflict among believers. First in this effort is to understanding God's order and placement of apostolic gifts. Consider the Apostle James. As the primary leader of the church in Jerusalem, he gave the final decision on areas of conflict and discussion. In Acts 15, the issues of imposing circumcision and the keeping of the Mosaic Law on the Gentiles arose and there was great debate between Paul and Barnabas. They brought these issues to the apostles and elders at Jerusalem and there was no quick decision. Instead there were hours and days of meals and fellowship and hearing one another's positions. And after much disputing, Peter spoke on behalf of the Gentiles (vv. 7–11) and then Paul and Barnabas testified of the miracles and wonders done among the Gentiles (v. 12). It was after exhaustive conversation and discussion and elaborate attempts to understand varied points of view that James spoke and gave his decision (vv. 13–20). All were pleased at his counsel and letters went out to inform the Gentiles of the commandment concerning them.

God releases gifts with the apostolic mandate. Even within the apostolic gifting diverse ranks exist. Rank exists in authority, produces judgment, government, order, harmony, and access to resources.

Here we make recommendation on how to resolve ministry conflict according to the level of relationship.

Other categories could include:
Pastor / Leader of the Ministry
1. Pastor or Leader with Leadership persons (Board Member or Elder or Deacon).
   This conflict could be over theological differences, could be strategic visions differences, could be financial issues, even domestic issues in family. Could be where Leader borrowed money and did not pay it back, or the other way around.
2. Pastor with a member of the congregation in conflict.
3. Leader (Board Member / Elder / Deacon / Department Leader) with a congregant.
4. Pastor with a member of staff in full-time employment.
5. Pastor with another Pastor in the city or Nation.
6. Pastor with an unbeliever.

7. Pastor with a political leader or political system.
8. Pastor in Conflict with his family (wife, children, parents, siblings, in-laws).
9. Pastor with health challenges.

Leadership in the ministry
1. Leaders in conflict with Pastor.
2. Leaders in conflict with another leader on the team.
3. Leader with a member of the congregation.
4. Leaders with another leader or member of another ministry.
5. Leaders that have conflict in their homes (family) marital conflict.
6. Leaders in conflict with their respective families.

Conflict in the Congregation
1. Member with another member.
2. Member in family conflicts.
3. Members in conflict with members of other ministries over business etc.

Other Categories
1. Sexual harassment.
2. Dismissal from employment and termination of services (volunteers).
3. Non-compliant members to vision, leadership, beliefs etc. of the ministry.

Dealing with unrelated conflicts
1. Conflict in another assembly other than your own.
   a. A church in the same fellowship whether they appeal for help or not.
   b. A church in the city or nation not in formal fellowship but the leader is a friend.
   c. A church in the city or nation where there are no connections or ties.
2. Conflict in church organizations that begin to experience church split or exodus of members.
   a. Within a ministry fellowship.

b. Ministries that are not related.

c. Dealing with the "rumors" in a city or nation concerning other ministers or ministries.

3. Conflict in church organizations as it pertains to property ownership, financial disputes.

a. Dealing with various forms of lawsuits against a ministry or within a ministry.

4. Disputes over elections as is the case in some ministries.

a. Disputes over successors and the process or lack of process.

5. Recommendations on various forms of disclaimers.

a. Offering / donations / gifts.

b. On investments where dividends are paid.

c. When television or radio or studio recordings are made.

d. Positions established as far as remunerations to volunteers on all levels.

e. Relationship expectations as they relate to leaders, members.

6. Conflict caused by leaders and/or members regarding political views and affiliations.

7. Conflict caused by racial tensions or cultural clashes from within and without.

8. Conflict caused thru theological era / differences.

Recommendations
- Establish code of conduct documentation
- Establish a process of dealing with conflict
- Establish accountability structures systems and a culture of accountability

CONGREGATION MEMBER VERSUS CHURCH LEADER

The following are areas of possible concern when avoiding conflict. First, depending on the impact of the conflict, it may be necessary to call in apostolic and pastoral oversight of the church. These are leaders the congregation knows who are known to have arbitration decision making authority.

Second, consider the spiritual influence of the conflict. Can this conflict be attributed to the atmosphere or region where the church is planted? Is this conflict a demonic attack that has the potential to hinder a move of God or damage the credibility of the church as a whole, or destroy a church completely?

Third, think about the social responsibility of the church relative to this conflict. If the ministry is located among businesses, do they stand to feel the impact of the conflict? Depending on the member's level of involvement in the ministry, look at how interaction with society is impacted by this conflict.

Next, look at all points of the economy, including the financial responsibility of the church. The question must be asked, how does this conflict influence the economy of the church? Conflict has a way of drying up a flow of finances that are needed and required to keep a ministry functioning and flourishing at a certain level.

I hold the position that God pays for His revival. God will ensure that for every vision there is ample financial provision and resource. If there is a stagnation of finances or difficulty in raising funds, then a church should begin to ask hard questions. Does God favor this particular event, building idea, program, etc? In my experience, if God births the vision, He sends the resources.

Finally, assess anointing levels. Is the worship level high and the prayer level low? Is the teaching level low and the preaching level high? Seek to achieve a balance in levels throughout the church.

CRAFTING APOSTOLIC DOCUMENTS

Apostolic documents protect not just the church, but all parties involved. They are written to ensure there are proper controls on the conflict resolution process. If the pastor is one of the parties engaged in the conflict, then an arbiter should be called in to facilitate the process. If there is no clarity of the actual dispute, then there will be a misjudgment.

All parties involved must agree to the following:

- Facts will be dealt with in an unbiased way.
- We will ignore personalities and only look at the principles, the facts.
- There must be a clear understanding of the arbiter's role on both sides, as well as an approved course of action.
- Before any judgments are passed, any teams to be formally and/or informally consulted will be presented on both sides.
- Express openness on both sides to constant counseling and redirection.

Apostolic documents help provide a guide for the process. It is not a short cut. Through consultation and discussion, the level of conflict that gets to this stage must be worked out over many weeks. Use Acts 15 as a model. There was a major conflict in the history of the church regarding Greek Christians and whether or not they were obligated to the Mosaic Law. The apostles dialogued over meals, over many weeks, to gain understanding. What is your position? What is your experience? What is God saying? It was not until there was thorough and sufficient understanding that James was prepared to offer his decision.

SIX: THE EXIT STRATEGY

"Care must be taken on how members of our ministry leave as this has great implications and possible consequences on the overall thrust of the ministry's core foundation."

Bishop Tudor Bismark

While they were worshipping the Lord and fasting, the Holy Spirit said, Separate now for Me Barnabas and Saul for the work to which I have called them. Then after fasting and praying, they put their hands on them and sent them away. So then, being sent out by the Holy Spirit, they went down to Seleusia, and from [that port] they sailed away to Cyprus.

Acts 13:2–4 (AMP)

First, let's define an exit. It is when an existing ministry member serving in any capacity critical to everyday operations resigns for the purposes of pursuing personal interests, to create a new ministry, or to change churches. While the reason for leaving plays a role in the process of exit or how the output of exit is to be achieved, the point of the exit strategy is to record the established protocol and order of the house (local church). Having an exit strategy in place makes transitions much easier.

A well planned exit approach from ministry significantly benefits both the ministry and the individual(s) concerned. Benefits to the ministry include the elimination of internal strife and rumor mongering, continued operational flow, intangible and tangible cost reduction, and the safe guarding of the ministry's interests and activities (with proper planning). Benefits to the individual are the blessing of the Father (the spiritual head of the house), contacts and/or resource support through various ministry departments or teams, and continued covering.

The correct exit strategy has four parts. First, identify the person's gift, measure the gift, develop time frames, assess demographics, and mentorship recommendations. Second, determine if the individual is in line with the service requirements of the ministry; find out where they have served in the church. Third, evaluate proficiencies in administration; find out if they are good with reporting; make sure there is an understanding of reporting systems and accountability. Finally, recommend support systems be developed around this person (people, finances, and certain assets). If this individual is unmarried, you want to set strong parameters and see certain manifestations of responsibility before they are sent out.

Every ministry or local church should have an exit strategy in place for extremely gifted persons and avoid potentially devastating situations. Develop a culture and make provision for the exit strategy. Be aware of the need for constant improvement. Allow structures and systems to be managed by individuals who can work through the processes. As soon as possible, implement the exit strategy.

Below is a brief outline of certain variables to consider when developing your exit strategy.

KNOW THE PEOPLE

The key to knowing people is asking questions. Ask direct questions that will give you clear answers. Make eye contact and be aware of "body language." Ask questions that will reveal their heart. Take note of their family, their friends, and their reputation in business, etc. Be clear and intentional in relationship with people. Know their goals, dreams, and passions.

BENEFITS

There are many reasons a person wants to leave the church. Having an exit strategy benefits both the ministry and the individual. For the ministry, the leader's vision, anointing and integrity are safeguarded. Internal strife and rumor mongering is eliminated. There is also a continuity of operations. For the individual, there is the blessing of the father, access to the father's resources and continual covering.

REVENUE FACTOR

At New Life Church in Harare, we do not send out pastors without proper training, exposure, and readiness assessments. We take practical steps. For example, we consider the pastoral candidates giving records. We investigate their financial records because of Biblical principle—one reaps what one sows. If the pastoral candidate was inconsistent in tithe, offering, and special giving, then he will reap members who are inconsistent in the same ways. If the candidate does not have a solid record, we offer the candidate time to stay in our fellowship and develop consistent giving patterns so that the ministry he plants will not struggle financially under a curse.

Second, we consider the demographics. Where is the location of the new church plant? What might we need to know about that area? What are the primary needs?

WHAT TO DO IF THERE IS NOT AN EXIT STRATEGY IN PLACE

Those desiring to leave should meet formally with pastors, make their intentions known, provide information about what they want to do, learn what it will take to leave, and follow up with documentation. Ideally, senior pastors will reciprocate with information.

But if they do not reciprocate, individuals should respond with a formal letter with a proposed date that they would like to be released and request blessing. Resend the letter if there is still no response. Ultimately, they can send a final letter with the date they will start the ministry.

A FINAL WORD

It is extremely vital that Ministries / Leaders have an understanding of the dynamics of conflict. Leaders must learn how to avoid, avert, prevent, direct, guide, and resolve conflicts. There are literally hundreds of ministries and ministers around the world in just about every country and culture, in various ages of time that have lost so much because of conflict. Many have lost their entire ministries, their reputation and credibility, and have caused unforeseen pain on many levels to many people due to conflicts that could have been prevented, or could have been dealt with in a reasonable way.

I have been in an Evangelical, Pentecostal, and Charismatic church for 37 years and have preached for 35 years and have seen so much heartbreak and division in the Body because of conflict. I have witnessed all kinds of conflicts that could have been avoided or could have been handled differently. Unfortunately so many hurts have been caused, and there have been numerous casualties. I have found that some leaders have lost everything, their marriage, their family, their health, their mind, their ministries and their future. I have felt for some time it would be meaningful to write something as a brief guide to help resolve problems, disputes, disagreements and controversies that create church splits. I have personally been involved in so many variations of conflict where we were required to resolve, arbitrate and contribute in resolving conflict, and have discovered that there were limited resources to assist in conflict resolution.

I wish to encourage that as part of our ministry development and training programs we teach conflict resolution. We need to establish conflict resolution as a key component in church culture so that the devil does not destroy our life's work through something that could have been avoided or perhaps handled in a better way. I admonish all leaders that do not have accountability structures and systems to establish them immediately. Neglecting the critical area of conflict resolution adds to the vulnerability that already plagues the body of Christ.

God's blessings to all, and may the Peace of God rule and reign in yours hearts, lives and ministries.

[1] www.merriam-webster.com, "conflict."
[2] www.merriam-webster.com, "drama."

CONFLICT RESOLUTION

LEADER'S GUIDE

DEALING WITH CONFLICT IN MINISTRY

LEADERSHIP
DEVELOPMENT GUIDE

CONTENTS

HOW TO BEST USE THIS LEADERSHIP GUIDE

SECTION ONE: THE DAVID MODEL (CAUSES OF CONFLICT)

Cause of Conflict – Sexual Sin
Cause of Conflict – Vision Issues
Cause of Conflict – Organizational Structures
Cause of Conflict – Family Conflict
Cause of Conflict – Lack of Maturity in the Body of Christ

SECTION TWO: THE JESUS MODEL (CONFLICT RESOLUTION)

Resolving Conflict – Succession Plan I (The 120)
Resolving Conflict – Succession Plan II (Apostle Paul)
Resolving Conflict – Transitional People (Philip)
Resolving Conflict – Permanent People (James and Peter)
Resolving Conflict – The Exit Strategy (Ascension)
Resolving Conflict – The Apostolic Document (John 17)

A FINAL WORD

HOW TO BEST USE THIS LEADERSHIP GUIDE

This guide resembles a study guide, but functions quite differently. As a *Leadership Guide*, it is designed to steer the reader in personal evaluation and study for the purpose of honing leadership skills.

Content in this guide does not directly mirror what you read in the *Conflict Resolution* booklet. The focus in this guide is conflict resolution so we will address biblical models and ask pointed questions to help the reader examine his own heart and service in the Kingdom of God.

Whether used together with the DVD sessions or the booklet, this Leadership Guide is designed to assist the reader in applying Bishop Bismark's recommended principles and in doing his or her own part to live peaceably with all men, as much as depends on them.

Each section in this *Guide* presents a biblical model in the following format:

1. Context—Scripture reference.
2. Overview of Biblical Model—Simple bulleted list of main points of biblical story.
3. Conflict(s) Presented—A short list of possible conflicts from the biblical story.
4. Leadership Development—Insightful meditation questions to help you search your heart and develop any weak areas of leadership.

Time parameters have not been set for this study—you may do the sections daily or weekly but we encourage an in-depth study of God's Word. Let His Word be the mirror for you first before you teach it to others.

We encourage you to complete every lesson, whether you feel it applies to you or not. It will still be profitable for you to complete the entire study as you will gain greater knowledge in the area of conflict resolution. Study the biblical records and allow the Holy Spirit to extract greater truths for you.

CONFLICT RESOLUTION

SECTION ONE: THE DAVID MODEL
LIVING WITH CONFLICT

And Samuel said to Saul, You have done foolishly! You have not kept the commandment of the Lord your God which He commanded you; for the Lord would have established your kingdom over Israel forever; but now your kingdom shall not continue; the Lord has sought out [David] a man after His own heart, and the Lord has commanded him to be prince and ruler over His people, because you have not kept what the Lord commanded you.

1 Samuel 13:13–14 (AMP)

SECTION ONE: THE DAVID MODEL
CAUSE OF CONFLICT – SEXUAL SIN

Context: 2 Samuel 11:1–13

¹And it came to pass, after the year was expired, at the time when kings go forth to battle, that David sent Joab, and his servants with him, and all Israel; and they destroyed the children of Ammon, and besieged Rabbah. But David tarried still at Jerusalem.

²And it came to pass in an eveningtide, that David arose from off his bed, and walked upon the roof of the king's house: and from the roof he saw a woman washing herself; and the woman was very beautiful to look upon.

³And David sent and enquired after the woman. And one said, Is not this Bathsheba, the daughter of Eliam, the wife of Uriah the Hittite?

⁴And David sent messengers, and took her; and she came in unto him, and he lay with her; for she was purified from her uncleanness: and she returned unto her house.

⁵And the woman conceived, and sent and told David, and said, I am with child.

⁶And David sent to Joab, saying, Send me Uriah the Hittite. And Joab sent Uriah to David.

⁷And when Uriah was come unto him, David demanded of him how Joab did, and how the people did, and how the war prospered.

⁸And David said to Uriah, Go down to thy house, and wash thy feet. And Uriah departed out of the king's house, and there followed him a mess of meat from the king.

⁹But Uriah slept at the door of the king's house with all the servants of his lord, and went not down to his house.

¹⁰And when they had told David, saying, Uriah went not down unto his house, David said unto Uriah, Camest thou not from thy journey? why then didst thou not go down unto thine house?

¹¹And Uriah said unto David, The ark, and Israel, and Judah, abide in tents; and my lord Joab, and the servants of my lord, are encamped in the open fields; shall I then go into mine house, to eat and to drink, and to lie with my wife? as thou livest, and as thy soul liveth, I will not do this thing.

¹²And David said to Uriah, Tarry here to day also, and to morrow I will let thee depart. So Uriah abode in Jerusalem that day, and the morrow.

¹³And when David had called him, he did eat and drink before him; and he made him drunk: and at even he went out to lie on his bed with the servants of his lord, but went not down to his house.

Summary/Overview

- The season called for battle, yet David sent his commander and servants and nation out to fight. He stayed home.
- David saw Bathsheba on the roof while on an evening stroll. She was bathing. He inquired about her, learning her name, her father's identity, and that she was married to Uriah, a member of his army.
- Using "executive privilege," David sent men to take Bathsheba. She was brought to him and he slept with her. She became pregnant and informed David.
- David called Uriah back from frontline battle and hoped he'd sleep with his wife. Instead he remained loyal in heart to his king and fellow soldiers and did not sleep with his wife.
- To further cover his sin, David sent Uriah back to battle with written instructions to place Uriah in the direct line of fire to be killed. Uriah died on the battlefield.
- David married Bathsheba. Their child died. They conceived again and had Solomon.

Conflict(s) Presented

- As a king, David is a leader. He had an assigned place, but chose to stay home.
- David, as the monarch, forced his way into Bathsheba's life, disobeying God and creating conflict in her house.
- Joab, following David's instructions, placed Uriah in the heat of battle to die.
- David set himself up for the same behavior to repeat itself in his family line. His behavior was a seed, later reaped in conflict with Absalom.

Leadership Development

- List all the behaviors that fall under the label of "sexual sin."

_____

_____

_____

• Considering David's story, who are all the people affected by his sin with Bathsheba?

_____

_____

_____

_____

• What was the real issue, or root, behind David's behavior?

_____

_____

_____

_____

• Why do you think forgiveness does not preclude experiencing consequences?

_____

_____

_____

_____

• Review your last three answers. Now, apply this to your ministry experience. Briefly describe an incident of Spiritual Sex Sin, where you violated a member of the Body of Christ, or you were violated spiritually.

_____

_____

_____

_____

• Stepping away from the people involved and the actual event, what was the real issue behind this experience?

_____

_____

_____

_____

• How many different *kinds* of people were affected? List them here.

_____

_____

_____

_____

• What were the consequences, whether or not this event became public knowledge?

_____

_____

_____

_____

SECTION ONE: THE DAVID MODEL
CAUSE OF CONFLICT – VISION ISSUES

Context: 1 Samuel 25: 2–13, 21–22

²And there was a man in Maon, whose possessions were in Carmel; and the man was very great, and he had three thousand sheep, and a thousand goats: and he was shearing his sheep in Carmel.

³Now the name of the man was Nabal; and the name of his wife Abigail: and she was a woman of good understanding, and of a beautiful countenance: but the man was churlish and evil in his doings; and he was of the house of Caleb.

⁴And David heard in the wilderness that Nabal did shear his sheep.

⁵And David sent out ten young men, and David said unto the young men, Get you up to Carmel, and go to Nabal, and greet him in my name:

⁶And thus shall ye say to him that liveth in prosperity, Peace be both to thee, and peace be to thine house, and peace be unto all that thou hast.

⁷And now I have heard that thou hast shearers: now thy shepherds which were with us, we hurt them not, neither was there ought missing unto them, all the while they were in Carmel.

⁸Ask thy young men, and they will shew thee. Wherefore let the young men find favour in thine eyes: for we come in a good day: give, I pray thee, whatsoever cometh to thine hand unto thy servants, and to thy son David.

⁹And when David's young men came, they spake to Nabal according to all those words in the name of David, and ceased.

¹⁰And Nabal answered David's servants, and said, Who is David? and who is the son of Jesse? there be many servants now a days that break away every man from his master.

¹¹Shall I then take my bread, and my water, and my flesh that I have killed for my shearers, and give it unto men, whom I know not whence they be?

¹²So David's young men turned their way, and went again, and came and told him all those sayings.

¹³And David said unto his men, Gird ye on every man his sword. And they girded on every man his sword; and David also girded on his sword: and there went up after David about four hundred men; and two hundred abode by the stuff.

²¹Now David had said, Surely in vain have I kept all that this fellow hath in

the wilderness, so that nothing was missed of all that pertained unto him: and he hath requited me evil for good.
[22]So and more also do God unto the enemies of David, if I leave of all that pertain to him by the morning light any that pisseth against the wall.

Summary/Overview

- Nabal and Abigail lived in Maon. During sheep shearing season, David sent messengers to Nabal requesting food for him and his men.
- David's message was not empty begging; he explained his worthiness to Nabal. In the wilderness neither David nor his men abused or stole from Nabal's shepherds.
- David referred to Nabal's young men as witnesses of him and his men's good behavior. He thought this merit enough to receive provisions.
- Nabal, whose name means fool, answered smugly against David, noting how there were many servants going AWOL from their masters. He used this as reason enough to deny David's request.
- When David's men recalled the encounter for him, he gave instructions to each of his men to put on their swords and prepare to fight.
- David was angry and felt he extended goodwill to Nabal's household in vain. He planned to kill every man on the property by the next morning.

Conflict(s) Presented

- David saw his request for food as an opportunity to forge relationship. As king, he would always remember Nabal's kindness.
- Nabal thought highly of himself and saw David's request as insulting, and David as unworthy. He insulted David and secured his fate.
- Nabal and David had a difference of opinion.

Leadership Development

• How was Nabal living out the meaning of his name?

_____

_____

_____

_____

• What was the conflict between Nabal and David?

_____

_____

_____

• When have you been a Nabal? Explain here.

_____

_____

_____

_____

• Did you have an Abigail to intercede and save life all around you?

_____

_____

_____

_____

• When have you been a David, and unjustly rejected? Explain here.

_____

_____

_____

_____

• What was your reaction? Was it similar to David's? Explain here.

_____

_____

_____

_____

SECTION ONE: THE DAVID MODEL
CAUSE OF CONFLICT – ORGANIZATIONAL
STRUCTURES

Context: 1 Chronicles 21

¹And Satan stood up against Israel, and provoked David to number Israel.

²And David said to Joab and to the rulers of the people, Go, number Israel from Beersheba even to Dan; and bring the number of them to me, that I may know it.

³And Joab answered, The LORD make his people an hundred times so many more as they be: but, my lord the king, are they not all my lord's servants? why then doth my lord require this thing? why will he be a cause of trespass to Israel?

⁴Nevertheless the king's word prevailed against Joab. Wherefore Joab departed, and went throughout all Israel, and came to Jerusalem.

⁵And Joab gave the sum of the number of the people unto David. And all they of Israel were a thousand thousand and an hundred thousand men that drew sword: and Judah was four hundred threescore and ten thousand men that drew sword.

⁶But Levi and Benjamin counted he not among them: for the king's word was abominable to Joab.

⁷And God was displeased with this thing; therefore he smote Israel.

⁸And David said unto God, I have sinned greatly, because I have done this thing: but now, I beseech thee, do away the iniquity of thy servant; for I have done very foolishly.

⁹And the LORD spake unto Gad, David's seer, saying,

¹⁰Go and tell David, saying, Thus saith the LORD, I offer thee three things: choose thee one of them, that I may do it unto thee.

¹¹So Gad came to David, and said unto him, Thus saith the LORD, Choose thee

¹²Either three years' famine; or three months to be destroyed before thy foes, while that the sword of thine enemies overtaketh thee; or else three days the sword of the LORD, even the pestilence, in the land, and the angel of the LORD destroying throughout all the coasts of Israel. Now therefore advise thyself what word I shall bring again to him that sent me.

¹³And David said unto Gad, I am in a great strait: let me fall now into the hand of the LORD; for very great are his mercies: but let me not fall into the hand of man.

¹⁴So the LORD sent pestilence upon Israel: and there fell of Israel seventy thousand men.

¹⁵And God sent an angel unto Jerusalem to destroy it: and as he was destroying, the LORD beheld, and he repented him of the evil, and said to the angel that destroyed, It is enough, stay now thine hand. And the angel of the LORD stood by the threshingfloor of Ornan the Jebusite.

¹⁶And David lifted up his eyes, and saw the angel of the LORD stand between the earth and the heaven, having a drawn sword in his hand stretched out over Jerusalem. Then David and the elders of Israel, who were clothed in sackcloth, fell upon their faces.

¹⁷And David said unto God, Is it not I that commanded the people to be numbered? even I it is that have sinned and done evil indeed; but as for these sheep, what have they done? let thine hand, I pray thee, O LORD my God, be on me, and on my father's house; but not on thy people, that they should be plagued.

¹⁸Then the angel of the LORD commanded Gad to say to David, that David should go up, and set up an altar unto the LORD in the threshingfloor of Ornan the Jebusite.

¹⁹And David went up at the saying of Gad, which he spake in the name of the LORD.

²⁰And Ornan turned back, and saw the angel; and his four sons with him hid themselves. Now Ornan was threshing wheat.

²¹And as David came to Ornan, Ornan looked and saw David, and went out of the threshingfloor, and bowed himself to David with his face to the ground.

²²Then David said to Ornan, Grant me the place of this threshingfloor, that I may build an altar therein unto the LORD: thou shalt grant it me for the full price: that the plague may be stayed from the people.

²³And Ornan said unto David, Take it to thee, and let my lord the king do that which is good in his eyes: lo, I give thee the oxen also for burnt offerings, and the threshing instruments for wood, and the wheat for the meat offering; I give it all.

²⁴And king David said to Ornan, Nay; but I will verily buy it for the full price: for I will not take that which is thine for the LORD, nor offer burnt offerings without cost.

[25]So David gave to Ornan for the place six hundred shekels of gold by weight.

[26]And David built there an altar unto the LORD, and offered burnt offerings and peace offerings, and called upon the LORD; and he answered him from heaven by fire upon the altar of burnt offering.

[27]And the LORD commanded the angel; and he put up his sword again into the sheath thereof.

[28]At that time when David saw that the LORD had answered him in the threshingfloor of Ornan the Jebusite, then he sacrificed there.

[29]For the tabernacle of the LORD, which Moses made in the wilderness, and the altar of the burnt offering, were at that season in the high place at Gibeon.

[30]But David could not go before it to enquire of God: for he was afraid because of the sword of the angel of the LORD.

Summary/Overview

- Satan provoked David to take a census. God already commanded David NOT to take a census. Joab offered caution and suggested David not take a census. David, as king, exercised royal privilege and overruled Joab's counsel.
- God struck Israel because He was displeased with David's action.
- David acknowledged his foolish action and asked God to take away His iniquity.
- Gad, David's prophet, gave David God's three options of penalties to choose from: three years of famine, three months to be defeated by enemies, or three days of pestilence in the land.
- David only asked to fall into the hands of God because of His great mercies.
- God sent an angel to destroy Jerusalem, but repented and changed His mind. David saw this angel standing by Ornan's threshing floor with a drawn sword stretched over Jerusalem. David and his elders repented in sackcloth and ashes.
- God sent a command through Gad for David to build an altar on Ornan's threshing floor. David obeyed and asked Ornan to give him his threshing floor to build an altar to the Lord to restrain the plague

and to name his price.

• Ornan would give David the threshing floor, but David bought it and offered burnt offerings and peace offerings. At the Lord's command, the angel put his sword back in its sheath.

Conflict(s) Presented

• God's perspective: Do not take the census. David's perspective: Take the census.
• David refused counsel and warning to take the census.
• Instead of an individual penalty from God, David took notice that the nation suffered for his disobedience.
• God did not want to issue judgment on the people; He gave David an out through sacrifice.

Leadership Development

• In what area(s) of ministry service have you made God your enemy through your disobedience to a known command? List here.

_____

_____

_____

_____

_____

_____

• Who was affected/judged because of your foolish decision?

_____

_____

_____

_____

• How did prophetic warning come?

_____

_____

_____

_____

• Did you repent? If so, under what circumstances?

_____

_____

_____

_____

• What did God require of you to satisfy Him?

_____

_____

_____

_____

SECTION ONE: THE DAVID MODEL CAUSE OF CONFLICT – FAMILY CONFLICT

Context: 2 Samuel 13

¹And it came to pass after this, that Absalom the son of David had a fair sister, whose name was Tamar; and Amnon the son of David loved her.

²And Amnon was so vexed, that he fell sick for his sister Tamar; for she was a virgin; and Amnon thought it hard for him to do anything to her.

³But Amnon had a friend, whose name was Jonadab, the son of Shimeah David's brother: and Jonadab was a very subtil man.

⁴And he said unto him, Why art thou, being the king's son, lean from day to day? wilt thou not tell me? And Amnon said unto him, I love Tamar, my brother Absalom's sister.

⁵And Jonadab said unto him, Lay thee down on thy bed, and make thyself sick: and when thy father cometh to see thee, say unto him, I pray thee, let my sister Tamar come, and give me meat, and dress the meat in my sight, that I may see it, and eat it at her hand.

⁶So Amnon lay down, and made himself sick: and when the king was come to see him, Amnon said unto the king, I pray thee, let Tamar my sister come, and make me a couple of cakes in my sight, that I may eat at her hand.

⁷Then David sent home to Tamar, saying, Go now to thy brother Amnon's house, and dress him meat.

⁸So Tamar went to her brother Amnon's house; and he was laid down. And she took flour, and kneaded it, and made cakes in his sight, and did bake the cakes.

⁹And she took a pan, and poured them out before him; but he refused to eat. And Amnon said, Have out all men from me. And they went out every man from him.

¹⁰And Amnon said unto Tamar, Bring the meat into the chamber, that I may eat of thine hand. And Tamar took the cakes which she had made, and brought them into the chamber to Amnon her brother.

¹¹And when she had brought them unto him to eat, he took hold of her, and said unto her, Come lie with me, my sister.

¹²And she answered him, Nay, my brother, do not force me; for no such thing ought to be done in Israel: do not thou this folly.

[13]And I, whither shall I cause my shame to go? and as for thee, thou shalt be as one of the fools in Israel. Now therefore, I pray thee, speak unto the king; for he will not withhold me from thee.

[14]Howbeit he would not hearken unto her voice: but, being stronger than she, forced her, and lay with her.

[15]Then Amnon hated her exceedingly; so that the hatred wherewith he hated her was greater than the love wherewith he had loved her. And Amnon said unto her, Arise, be gone.

[16]And she said unto him, There is no cause: this evil in sending me away is greater than the other that thou didst unto me. But he would not hearken unto her.

[17]Then he called his servant that ministered unto him, and said, Put now this woman out from me, and bolt the door after her.

[18]And she had a garment of divers colours upon her: for with such robes were the king's daughters that were virgins apparelled. Then his servant brought her out, and bolted the door after her.

[19]And Tamar put ashes on her head, and rent her garment of divers colours that was on her, and laid her hand on her head, and went on crying.

[20]And Absalom her brother said unto her, Hath Amnon thy brother been with thee? but hold now thy peace, my sister: he is thy brother; regard not this thing. So Tamar remained desolate in her brother Absalom's house.

[21]But when king David heard of all these things, he was very wroth.

[22]And Absalom spake unto his brother Amnon neither good nor bad: for Absalom hated Amnon, because he had forced his sister Tamar.

[23]And it came to pass after two full years, that Absalom had sheepshearers in Baalhazor, which is beside Ephraim: and Absalom invited all the king's sons.

[24]And Absalom came to the king, and said, Behold now, thy servant hath sheepshearers; let the king, I beseech thee, and his servants go with thy servant.

[25]And the king said to Absalom, Nay, my son, let us not all now go, lest we be chargeable unto thee. And he pressed him: howbeit he would not go, but blessed him.

[26]Then said Absalom, If not, I pray thee, let my brother Amnon go with us. And the king said unto him, Why should he go with thee?

[27]But Absalom pressed him, that he let Amnon and all the king's sons go

with him.

²⁸Now Absalom had commanded his servants, saying, Mark ye now when Amnon's heart is merry with wine, and when I say unto you, Smite Amnon; then kill him, fear not: have not I commanded you? be courageous, and be valiant.

²⁹And the servants of Absalom did unto Amnon as Absalom had commanded. Then all the king's sons arose, and every man gat him up upon his mule, and fled.

³⁰And it came to pass, while they were in the way, that tidings came to David, saying, Absalom hath slain all the king's sons, and there is not one of them left.

³¹Then the king arose, and tare his garments, and lay on the earth; and all his servants stood by with their clothes rent.

³²And Jonadab, the son of Shimeah David's brother, answered and said, Let not my lord suppose that they have slain all the young men the king's sons; for Amnon only is dead: for by the appointment of Absalom this hath been determined from the day that he forced his sister Tamar.

³³Now therefore let not my lord the king take the thing to his heart, to think that all the king's sons are dead: for Amnon only is dead.

³⁴But Absalom fled. And the young man that kept the watch lifted up his eyes, and looked, and, behold, there came much people by the way of the hill side behind him.

³⁵And Jonadab said unto the king, Behold, the king's sons come: as thy servant said, so it is.

³⁶And it came to pass, as soon as he had made an end of speaking, that, behold, the king's sons came, and lifted up their voice and wept: and the king also and all his servants wept very sore.

³⁷But Absalom fled, and went to Talmai, the son of Ammihud, king of Geshur. And David mourned for his son every day.

³⁸So Absalom fled, and went to Geshur, and was there three years.

³⁹And the soul of king David longed to go forth unto Absalom: for he was comforted concerning Amnon, seeing he was dead.

Summary/Overview

- Amnon seduced and raped his half-sister Tamar. Absalom, her full brother, comforted Tamar and sent her to live in his house.
- David was quiet on this matter.

57

- Absalom pretended for two years that the matter was settled while all the while planning to assassinate Amnon. After he killed his brother he fled to his grandfather's kingdom.
- David grieved Amnon's death, and did not punish Absalom.

Conflict(s) Presented

- Tamar, the king's daughter, was raped by her half-brother Amnon. Her father David, the king, did not defend her nor did he chastise Amnon.
- Absalom secretly harbored unforgiveness against Amnon and waited two years before implementing a plot to kill him.
- David did not avenge Amnon.

Leadership Development

- Consider this story in a current-day ministry setting. Identify when you were in the role of Tamar, Amnon and/or Absalom.

_____

_____

_____

_____

_____

- We do not have a scriptural record, but if you were any of the children of David, how would your relationship with him have changed? How was the relationship with your spiritual father affected by your ministry experience?

_____

_____

_____

_____

- Why do you believe David (your spiritual father) should avenge you?

_____

_____

_____

_____

• Have you ever separated from a ministry on "bad terms" because of family conflict?

_____

_____

_____

_____

• What would it take for you to let it go and move on?

_____

_____

_____

_____

• What are the cause and effects to a ministry with passive leadership?

_____

_____

_____

_____

SECTION ONE: THE DAVID MODEL
CAUSE OF CONFLICT –
LACK OF MATURITY IN BODY OF CHRIST

Context: 2 Samuel 16:5–14 and 19:8–23

⁵And when king David came to Bahurim, behold, thence came out a man of the family of the house of Saul, whose name was Shimei, the son of Gera: he came forth, and cursed still as he came.

⁶And he cast stones at David, and at all the servants of king David: and all the people and all the mighty men were on his right hand and on his left.

⁷And thus said Shimei when he cursed, Come out, come out, thou bloody man, and thou man of Belial:

⁸The LORD hath returned upon thee all the blood of the house of Saul, in whose stead thou hast reigned; and the LORD hath delivered the kingdom into the hand of Absalom thy son: and, behold, thou art taken in thy mischief, because thou art a bloody man.

⁹Then said Abishai the son of Zeruiah unto the king, Why should this dead dog curse my lord the king? let me go over, I pray thee, and take off his head.

¹⁰And the king said, What have I to do with you, ye sons of Zeruiah? so let him curse, because the LORD hath said unto him, Curse David. Who shall then say, Wherefore hast thou done so?

¹¹And David said to Abishai, and to all his servants, Behold, my son, which came forth of my bowels, seeketh my life: how much more now may this Benjamite do it? let him alone, and let him curse; for the LORD hath bidden him.

¹²It may be that the LORD will look on mine affliction, and that the LORD will requite me good for his cursing this day.

¹³And as David and his men went by the way, Shimei went along on the hill's side over against him, and cursed as he went, and threw stones at him, and cast dust.

¹⁴And the king, and all the people that were with him, came weary, and refreshed themselves there.

19:8–23

⁸Then the king arose, and sat in the gate. And they told unto all the people, saying, Behold, the king doth sit in the gate. And all the people came before the king: for Israel had fled every man to his tent.

⁹And all the people were at strife throughout all the tribes of Israel, saying, The king saved us out of the hand of our enemies, and he delivered us out of the hand of the Philistines; and now he is fled out of the land for Absalom.

¹⁰And Absalom, whom we anointed over us, is dead in battle. Now therefore why speak ye not a word of bringing the king back?

¹¹And king David sent to Zadok and to Abiathar the priests, saying, Speak unto the elders of Judah, saying, Why are ye the last to bring the king back to his house? seeing the speech of all Israel is come to the king, even to his house.

¹²Ye are my brethren, ye are my bones and my flesh: wherefore then are ye the last to bring back the king?

¹³And say ye to Amasa, Art thou not of my bone, and of my flesh? God do so to me, and more also, if thou be not captain of the host before me continually in the room of Joab.

¹⁴And he bowed the heart of all the men of Judah, even as the heart of one man; so that they sent this word unto the king, Return thou, and all thy servants.

¹⁵So the king returned, and came to Jordan. And Judah came to Gilgal, to go to meet the king, to conduct the king over Jordan.

¹⁶And Shimei the son of Gera, a Benjamite, which was of Bahurim, hasted and came down with the men of Judah to meet king David.

¹⁷And there were a thousand men of Benjamin with him, and Ziba the servant of the house of Saul, and his fifteen sons and his twenty servants with him; and they went over Jordan before the king.

¹⁸And there went over a ferry boat to carry over the king's household, and to do what he thought good. And Shimei the son of Gera fell down before the king, as he was come over Jordan;

¹⁹And said unto the king, Let not my lord impute iniquity unto me, neither do thou remember that which thy servant did perversely the day that my lord the king went out of Jerusalem, that the king should take it to his heart.

²⁰For thy servant doth know that I have sinned: therefore, behold, I am come the first this day of all the house of Joseph to go down to meet my lord the king.

²¹But Abishai the son of Zeruiah answered and said, Shall not Shimei be put to death for this, because he cursed the LORD's anointed?
²²And David said, What have I to do with you, ye sons of Zeruiah, that ye should this day be adversaries unto me? shall there any man be put to death this day in Israel? for do not I know that I am this day king over Israel?
²³Therefore the king said unto Shimei, Thou shalt not die. And the king sware unto him.

Summary/Overview
- Shimei was a descendant of Saul. He threw stones and cursed David and David's men. He shouted judgments at David regarding Absalom's kingdom takeover.
- David would not let Abishai kill Shimei. David allowed Shimei to live and continue shouting curses in case the Lord sent him to release curses.
- As long as David continued walking with his men, Shimei walked parallel to them shouting curses and throwing stones.
- When David was reestablished as king, Shimei hurried to meet David when he arrived back in Jerusalem. Shimei asked that his curse-spouting and stone-throwing not be taken to heart by David because he knew he sinned.
- Abishai wanted to put Shimei to death. David wanted to sit as king again with no one dying that day. David swore to Shimei he would not die.

Conflict(s) Presented
- Shimei acted out of emotion and demonstrated immaturity.
- Shimei acted alone; he thought he was defending the house of Saul.
- Shimei had unfounded resentment against David.

Leadership Development
- Consider your early years of salvation. How many times have you been Shimei, secretly or publicly? List below.

_____

_____

_____

_____

_____

• Did you repent to "David"? How?

_____

_____

_____

_____

_____

_____

_____

• Did David release your sin and "let you live" or did he curse you in return?

_____

_____

_____

_____

• What do you take away from this story?

_____

_____

_____

_____

CONFLICT RESOLUTION

SECTION TWO: THE JESUS MODEL
RESOLVING CONFLICT – SUCCESSION PLAN

For the Son of Man is not come to destroy men's lives, but to save them.

Luke 9:56a (KJV)

I came that they might have and enjoy life, and have it in abundance (to the full, till it overflows).

John 10:10b (AMP)

The Son of God appeared for this purpose, to destroy the works of the devil.

1 John 3:8b (NAS)

For the Son of Man came to seek and to save that which was lost.

Luke 19:10 (AMP)

SECTION TWO: THE JESUS MODEL RESOLVING CONFLICT – SUCCESSION PLAN I (THE 120)

Context: Acts 1:8 – 2:13

[8]*But ye shall receive power, after that the Holy Ghost is come upon you: and ye shall be witnesses unto me both in Jerusalem, and in all Judaea, and in Samaria, and unto the uttermost part of the earth.*

[9]*And when he had spoken these things, while they beheld, he was taken up; and a cloud received him out of their sight.*

[10]*And while they looked stedfastly toward heaven as he went up, behold, two men stood by them in white apparel;*

[11]*Which also said, Ye men of Galilee, why stand ye gazing up into heaven? this same Jesus, which is taken up from you into heaven, shall so come in like manner as ye have seen him go into heaven.*

[12]*Then returned they unto Jerusalem from the mount called Olivet, which is from Jerusalem a sabbath day's journey.*

[13]*And when they were come in, they went up into an upper room, where abode both Peter, and James, and John, and Andrew, Philip, and Thomas, Bartholomew, and Matthew, James the son of Alphaeus, and Simon Zelotes, and Judas the brother of James.*

[14]*These all continued with one accord in prayer and supplication, with the women, and Mary the mother of Jesus, and with his brethren.*

[15]*And in those days Peter stood up in the midst of the disciples, and said, (the number of names together were about an hundred and twenty,)*

[16]*Men and brethren, this scripture must needs have been fulfilled, which the Holy Ghost by the mouth of David spake before concerning Judas, which was guide to them that took Jesus.*

[17]*For he was numbered with us, and had obtained part of this ministry.*

[18]*Now this man purchased a field with the reward of iniquity; and falling headlong, he burst asunder in the midst, and all his bowels gushed out.*

[19]*And it was known unto all the dwellers at Jerusalem; insomuch as that field is called in their proper tongue, Aceldama, that is to say, The field of blood.*

[20]*For it is written in the book of Psalms, Let his habitation be desolate, and*

let no man dwell therein: and his bishoprick let another take.

[21]Wherefore of these men which have companied with us all the time that the Lord Jesus went in and out among us,

[22]Beginning from the baptism of John, unto that same day that he was taken up from us, must one be ordained to be a witness with us of his resurrection.

[23]And they appointed two, Joseph called Barsabas, who was surnamed Justus, and Matthias.

[24]And they prayed, and said, Thou, Lord, which knowest the hearts of all men, shew whether of these two thou hast chosen,

[25]That he may take part of this ministry and apostleship, from which Judas by transgression fell, that he might go to his own place.

[26]And they gave forth their lots; and the lot fell upon Matthias; and he was numbered with the eleven apostles.

2:1–13

[1]And when the day of Pentecost was fully come, they were all with one accord in one place.

[2]And suddenly there came a sound from heaven as of a rushing mighty wind, and it filled all the house where they were sitting.

[3]And there appeared unto them cloven tongues like as of fire, and it sat upon each of them.

[4]And they were all filled with the Holy Ghost, and began to speak with other tongues, as the Spirit gave them utterance.

[5]And there were dwelling at Jerusalem Jews, devout men, out of every nation under heaven.

[6]Now when this was noised abroad, the multitude came together, and were confounded, because that every man heard them speak in his own language.

[7]And they were all amazed and marvelled, saying one to another, Behold, are not all these which speak Galilaeans?

[8]And how hear we every man in our own tongue, wherein we were born?

[9]Parthians, and Medes, and Elamites, and the dwellers in Mesopotamia, and in Judaea, and Cappadocia, in Pontus, and Asia,

[10]Phrygia, and Pamphylia, in Egypt, and in the parts of Libya about Cyrene, and strangers of Rome, Jews and proselytes,

[11]Cretes and Arabians, we do hear them speak in our tongues the wonderful works of God.

[12]And they were all amazed, and were in doubt, saying one to another, What meaneth this?
[13]Others mocking said, These men are full of new wine.

Summary/Overview
- Jesus promised the power of the Holy Ghost to witness locally, regionally, nationally, and around the world and then ascended on a cloud.
- The disciples and others gathered in an upper room to await the promise of the Holy Spirit.
- They chose Matthias as the disciple in Judas' place.
- The day of Pentecost came and they (the 120) were all together in one place.
- In this one place they were all in one accord.
- Suddenly the sound like a wind came and cloven tongues of fire sat on all in the upper room and they were filled with the Holy Ghost.
- The people in the streets heard and understood the works of God in their own languages.

Conflict(s) Resolved
- Peter arose as an apostolic leader among the eleven remaining disciples in leading the selection process of Judas' replacement.
- The leadership government remained intact with Matthias selected as the new twelfth apostle.
- The disciples transitioned into apostles, suggesting that the void of necessary leadership was now filled in them.
- The Gospel message contained in the upper room with the 120, was concentrated, focused, and purified through extended prayer, worship and waiting on the Holy Spirit.
- When the works of God were heard and understood in other languages, a portal opened for the distribution of the Gospel message.

Leadership Development

• Do you remember receiving your call or divine assignment from God? Explain here.

_____
_____
_____
_____
_____

• Who was there?

_____
_____
_____
_____

• Describe any early experiences in team ministry.

_____
_____
_____
_____
_____

• What is the Message you carry?

_____
_____
_____
_____
_____

CONFLICT RESOLUTION

• What part do you play in spreading the Gospel message?

_____

_____

_____

_____

_____

SECTION TWO: THE JESUS MODEL RESOLVING CONFLICT – SUCCESSION PLAN II (PAUL)

Context: Acts 26:12–18

¹²Whereupon as I went to Damascus with authority and commission from the chief priests,

¹³At midday, O king, I saw in the way a light from heaven, above the brightness of the sun, shining round about me and them which journeyed with me.

¹⁴And when we were all fallen to the earth, I heard a voice speaking unto me, and saying in the Hebrew tongue, Saul, Saul, why persecutest thou me? it is hard for thee to kick against the pricks.

¹⁵And I said, Who art thou, Lord? And he said, I am Jesus whom thou persecutest.

¹⁶But rise, and stand upon thy feet: for I have appeared unto thee for this purpose, to make thee a minister and a witness both of these things which thou hast seen, and of those things in the which I will appear unto thee;

¹⁷Delivering thee from the people, and from the Gentiles, unto whom now I send thee,

¹⁸To open their eyes, and to turn them from darkness to light, and from the power of Satan unto God, that they may receive forgiveness of sins, and inheritance among them which are sanctified by faith that is in me.

Summary/Overview

- Paul recounts for King Agrippa his experience with Jesus the Messiah on the road to Damascus.
- Paul's purpose for receiving this revelation was to be appointed a minister and witness to what he had seen and what he would be shown by Jesus.
- Paul was rescued from the Jews and sent to the Gentiles.
- Paul's assignment to the Gentiles: to open their eyes so they may turn from darkness to light and from the domination of Satan to God.
- The desire of Christ was for the Gentiles to receive forgiveness of sins and an inheritance among those sanctified by faith in Him.

71

Conflict(s) Resolved
- Gentiles were positioned to become friends of God through relationship with Jesus Christ.
- In calling Paul, Jesus created a bridge for the Gentiles to cross over from darkness and satanic influence to light and God possession.

Leadership Development
- How have you personally benefited by Paul's assignment to Gentiles?

_____

_____

_____

_____

_____

_____

- Do you know of someone or of some ministry that is called to a people group like Paul?

_____

_____

_____

_____

- What does Jesus provide for the Gentiles?

_____

_____

_____

_____

_____

- In ministry, what is your calling to other races and ethnicities?

_____

_____
_____
_____
_____

• What does it mean to you to have a ministry that "goes to the nations"?

_____
_____
_____
_____

SECTION TWO: THE JESUS MODEL RESOLVING CONFLICT – TRANSITIONAL PEOPLE (PHILIP)

Context: Acts 8:1–8

¹And Saul was consenting unto his death. And at that time there was a great persecution against the church which was at Jerusalem; and they were all scattered abroad throughout the regions of Judaea and Samaria, except the apostles.

²And devout men carried Stephen to his burial, and made great lamentation over him.

³As for Saul, he made havock of the church, entering into every house, and haling men and women committed them to prison.

⁴Therefore they that were scattered abroad went every where preaching the word.

⁵Then Philip went down to the city of Samaria, and preached Christ unto them.

⁶And the people with one accord gave heed unto those things which Philip spake, hearing and seeing the miracles which he did.

⁷For unclean spirits, crying with loud voice, came out of many that were possessed with them: and many taken with palsies, and that were lame, were healed.

⁸And there was great joy in that city.

Summary/Overview

- The church in Jerusalem suffered persecution and all but the apostles were scattered.
- Stephen was buried.
- Saul started destroying the church.
- Those scattered preached the Word wherever they went.
- Philip went to Samaria and proclaimed Christ to them.
- The people paid attention to Philip as they heard and saw the signs he performed.
- Many were delivered from unclean spirits. Paralytics and the lame were healed. There was much rejoicing in Samaria.

- Philip was ordained a deacon to serve Grecian and Hebraic Jews. In the scattering, he became an evangelist.
- Circumstances caused Philip to step up in his function and move from Jerusalem.

Conflict(s) Resolved

- The Gospel was shared because of Philip's obedience.
- An influential man—eunuch to Queen Candace—was born again and carried his new faith back to his region.
- A trained leader was ready to move when God spoke to him.

Leadership Development

- Think of a time when you simply obeyed God to minister to another person, like the Ethiopian eunuch. Briefly describe.

_____

_____

_____

_____

- How did you facilitate your own transition out of a local body and into God's chosen ministry for you?

_____

_____

_____

_____

- Are you able to recognize those in ministry ready for promotion?

_____

_____

_____

_____

• What measures do you take to transition a deacon into an elder?

_____

_____

_____

_____

_____

• What is the purpose of ordaining deacons and elders for the church of God?

_____

_____

_____

_____

_____

SECTION TWO: THE JESUS MODEL RESOLVING CONFLICT – PERMANENT PEOPLE (JAMES & PETER)

Context: Luke 9:28–36

[28]And it came to pass about an eight days after these sayings, he took Peter and John and James, and went up into a mountain to pray.

[29]And as he prayed, the fashion of his countenance was altered, and his raiment was white and glistering.

[30]And, behold, there talked with him two men, which were Moses and Elias:

[31]Who appeared in glory, and spake of his decease which he should accomplish at Jerusalem.

[32]But Peter and they that were with him were heavy with sleep: and when they were awake, they saw his glory, and the two men that stood with him.

[33]And it came to pass, as they departed from him, Peter said unto Jesus, Master, it is good for us to be here: and let us make three tabernacles; one for thee, and one for Moses, and one for Elias: not knowing what he said.

[34]While he thus spake, there came a cloud, and overshadowed them: and they feared as they entered into the cloud.

[35]And there came a voice out of the cloud, saying, This is my beloved Son: hear him.

[36]And when the voice was past, Jesus was found alone. And they kept it close, and told no man in those days any of those things which they had seen.

Summary/Overview

- Jesus took Peter, John and James and went up into a mountain to pray.
- Jesus changed in outward show as He prayed and Moses and Elijah appeared.
- Peter, John and James awoke from heavy sleep to witness Jesus, Moses and Elijah talking about Jesus' soon coming death.
- Peter proposed to make three tabernacles—one for Jesus, Moses and Elijah.

- While Peter spoke a cloud overshadowed them and they heard the voice say, "This is my beloved Son: hear him."
- After the voice Jesus was alone. Peter, John, and James did not share what they witnessed.

Conflict(s) Resolved

- Jesus, through exposure to His glory, now had people to manage the movement of Christianity in the world.
- James provided decision-making leadership for Jewish Believers and was a pillar to the early church (Acts 12:17).
- Peter's influence opened up to witness the salvation of Gentiles (Acts 2:14).

Leadership Development

- Are you now or have you ever been a person on which ministry was built? If so, who do you think you are most like—Peter, John or James?

_____

_____

_____

_____

- As a senior leader, how do you gauge who is permanently fixed in the ministry?

_____

_____

_____

_____

- What is Peter's dominant trait that makes him a foundation person?

_____

_____

_____

_____

• What is John's major quality?

_____

_____

_____

• What is James' strength that makes him a person on which a ministry could be built?

_____

_____

_____

_____

_____

SECTION TWO: THE JESUS MODEL RESOLVING CONFLICT – THE EXIT STRATEGY

Context: Acts 1:4–11

⁴And, being assembled together with them, commanded them that they should not depart from Jerusalem, but wait for the promise of the Father, which, saith he, ye have heard of me.

⁵For John truly baptized with water; but ye shall be baptized with the Holy Ghost not many days hence.

⁶When they therefore were come together, they asked of him, saying, Lord, wilt thou at this time restore again the kingdom to Israel?

⁷And he said unto them, It is not for you to know the times or the seasons, which the Father hath put in his own power.

⁸But ye shall receive power, after that the Holy Ghost is come upon you: and ye shall be witnesses unto me both in Jerusalem, and in all Judaea, and in Samaria, and unto the uttermost part of the earth.

⁹And when he had spoken these things, while they beheld, he was taken up; and a cloud received him out of their sight.

¹⁰And while they looked stedfastly toward heaven as he went up, behold, two men stood by them in white apparel;

¹¹Which also said, Ye men of Galilee, why stand ye gazing up into heaven? this same Jesus, which is taken up from you into heaven, shall so come in like manner as ye have seen him go into heaven.

Summary/Overview

- Jesus gave command to remain in Jerusalem and wait on the promise of the Holy Ghost.
- Wondering about the ministry transition, the gathered group asked if the time had come for Jesus to restore the kingdom to Israel.
- Jesus emphasized their receiving the power of the Holy Ghost to be witnesses.
- As they watched, Jesus was taken up and received by a cloud out of their sight.
- They looked intently toward heaven as Jesus ascended.

• Two men dressed in white appeared and asked why they gazed into heaven.

Conflict(s) Resolved

• Jesus needed no one to complete His earthly assignment. The redemptive work was done.
• No one needed to be another Jesus, only to spread the Message.
• The kingdom was conferred to those who gathered and later received the power of the Holy Ghost.
• There was no argument about succeeding Jesus; He properly equipped enough men and women to continue His legacy.

Leadership Development

• What is your philosophy about leaving a ministry or local church?

_____

_____

_____

_____

• As a senior leader, do you have an exit strategy in place where you serve?

_____

_____

_____

_____

• How many ministry separations have you personally encountered?

_____

_____

_____

_____

• What did you learn each time?

_____

_____

_____

_____

• Evaluate how you left ministry. Were there witnesses to your work, to the completion of your assignment?

_____

_____

_____

_____

• What do you take from Jesus' ascension model when leaving ministry?

_____

_____

_____

_____

SECTION TWO: THE JESUS MODEL RESOLVING CONFLICT – THE APOSTOLIC DOCUMENT

Context: John 17

¹These words spake Jesus, and lifted up his eyes to heaven, and said, Father, the hour is come; glorify thy Son, that thy Son also may glorify thee:

²As thou hast given him power over all flesh, that he should give eternal life to as many as thou hast given him.

³And this is life eternal, that they might know thee the only true God, and Jesus Christ, whom thou hast sent.

⁴I have glorified thee on the earth: I have finished the work which thou gavest me to do.

⁵And now, O Father, glorify thou me with thine own self with the glory which I had with thee before the world was.

⁶I have manifested thy name unto the men which thou gavest me out of the world: thine they were, and thou gavest them me; and they have kept thy word.

⁷Now they have known that all things whatsoever thou hast given me are of thee.

⁸For I have given unto them the words which thou gavest me; and they have received them, and have known surely that I came out from thee, and they have believed that thou didst send me.

⁹I pray for them: I pray not for the world, but for them which thou hast given me; for they are thine.

¹⁰And all mine are thine, and thine are mine; and I am glorified in them.

¹¹And now I am no more in the world, but these are in the world, and I come to thee. Holy Father, keep through thine own name those whom thou hast given me, that they may be one, as we are.

¹²While I was with them in the world, I kept them in thy name: those that thou gavest me I have kept, and none of them is lost, but the son of perdition; that the scripture might be fulfilled.

¹³And now come I to thee; and these things I speak in the world, that they might have my joy fulfilled in themselves.

¹⁴I have given them thy word; and the world hath hated them, because they are not of the world, even as I am not of the world.

[15]I pray not that thou shouldest take them out of the world, but that thou shouldest keep them from the evil.

[16]They are not of the world, even as I am not of the world.

[17]Sanctify them through thy truth: thy word is truth.

[18]As thou hast sent me into the world, even so have I also sent them into the world.

[19]And for their sakes I sanctify myself, that they also might be sanctified through the truth.

[20]Neither pray I for these alone, but for them also which shall believe on me through their word;

[21]That they all may be one; as thou, Father, art in me, and I in thee, that they also may be one in us: that the world may believe that thou hast sent me.

[22]And the glory which thou gavest me I have given them; that they may be one, even as we are one:

[23]I in them, and thou in me, that they may be made perfect in one; and that the world may know that thou hast sent me, and hast loved them, as thou hast loved me.

[24]Father, I will that they also, whom thou hast given me, be with me where I am; that they may behold my glory, which thou hast given me: for thou lovedst me before the foundation of the world.

[25]O righteous Father, the world hath not known thee: but I have known thee, and these have known that thou hast sent me.

[26]And I have declared unto them thy name, and will declare it: that the love wherewith thou hast loved me may be in them, and I in them.

Summary/Overview

- Known as the high priestly prayer, Jesus prays for one thing and two groups of people: for God to be glorified, His disciples, and the church. Jesus expresses His final wishes for the care of current and future disciples.
- Jesus defines eternal life, to know God. He commended the disciples' understanding, saying that they came to know God as He was the source of all that came from Jesus.
- He prays for the disciples: joy made full, to be kept from evil one, sanctify in word of truth, sent into the world, and oneness.

• Jesus prays for His entire body (present and future): give them glory and make them one, and let them be where He is.

Conflict(s) Resolved

• Jesus in this prayer revealed the Father's heart for the Body – oneness.
• The Body has clarity on how their life in Christ should look in the earth.
• Even demonic oppression is put in its place.

Leadership Development

• How does your life match up with John 17? Explain here.

_____

_____

_____

_____

_____

• Explain the difference between a member and a disciple?

_____

_____

_____

_____

• What did Jesus define as a disciple?

_____

_____

_____

_____

_____

CONFLICT RESOLUTION

OTHER RESOURCES FROM BISHOP TUDOR BISMARK (OR TBM)

Suggested: Conflict Resolution, Spirit of Honor and Order of the Kingdom CD & DVD albums.

Please contact us:

Tudor Bismark Ministries, P. O. Box 58966, London, SE6 9HB

+44 (0) 20 8461 2414 / 03330 8 TUDOR (0333 0888 367)

Mail@TudorBismark.org.uk

www.TudorBismark.org.uk

CONFLICT RESOLUTION

94883063R00049